Girlfriend material:Signs that reveals She is an Ideal Sweetheart Material.

By Valentine Smith

Table of content

Introduction

I believe that a woman is the perfect girlfriend if she is intelligent without being intimidating, kind and considerate, and obviously fantastic in bed. However, that is only one woman's perception of what it takes to be a good girlfriend; you might be surprised to learn what men think.

It can be tempting to try and alter yourself in order to become girlfriend material if you're single and concerned that no one thinks you're attractive enough. Avoid doing this. What a man perceives as being less than ideal about one woman may make her into a queen in another man's eyes.

However, if you're interested in learning what men think makes a woman "girlfriend material" and how to be a good girlfriend, you're in luck because the men of the AskMen forum are back to share their opinions—both positive and negative—on what it takes to be a woman.

No man is an island, as cliché as that statement may sound. We eventually tire of putting ourselves out there after numerous first dates and frequent night outs and hope that she will be "the one." At the end of the day, maybe what we really want is someone who will be there for us every day, without fail.

Unfortunately, it doesn't come easy. One tricky part of the dating cycle is knowing when to transition from casually going out and getting to know each other to officially being in a relationship.

Chapter 1

Here are signs that can help you determine whether the woman that you're currently seeing is a keeper who is worthy of your time and efforts.

She loves and accepts you for who you are

Love means taking everything in –the good, the bad, and the unknown. Being with someone who accepts you for who you are will make you more comfortable and at ease to show your true personality. We all have flaws, just like any other normal human being. And being with a loving woman means that you are respected, despite any flaws you may have. A good partner would never attempt to force you to conform to a particular set of standards. Being with a woman you can be crazy with without worrying about being judged or looked down upon is another telltale sign of being with someone for the long haul.

You genuinely believe she is funny and cool.

When asked why you love someone, if you are unable to name even one non-physical quality, you may simply be smitten with the thought of always having a companion. A great sense of humor will undoubtedly endure the test of time while good looks fade. A person with a great sense of humor is like a breath of fresh air, and they will undoubtedly be able to find the positive in any circumstance. Building a solid relationship starts with finding people who have similar interests and outlooks on life. One sign that the woman you're dating is a potential girlfriend is if she spends a lot of time hanging out and talking to you.

She engages in open dialogue

She speaks her mind without fear, like a strong, independent woman. She doesn't expect you to be able to read her mind without her having to say anything; instead, she shares her thoughts and feelings with you. A good partner must have the guts to always be honest, refusing to sugarcoat anything in an effort to make you feel good for the wrong reasons. She is also old enough to understand that it is detrimental to a relationship to play mind games and act in ways that will only serve to enrage her partner.

She carries herself well

A confident woman simply goes to show that she embraces, and she fully accepts herself. Being with someone who loathes herself can be very draining. You don't want to spend most of your time reassuring her constantly that she's pretty, intelligent or in any other way enough for you. A confident woman is not an attention-whore who seeks validation for every single thing. Overall, her feminine demeanour also includes dressing up decently, without ever feeling the need to dress in extra tight, shiny, and skimpy clothes just to attract attention.

She respects your faith, family, and friends

You might try to rationalise this in the earlier phases, but this will surely lead to more complications down the road. These are the three Fs that cannot be compromised upon in a relationship. A relationship must be built on a strong foundation, and respecting each other's beliefs plays a role of paramount importance in a smooth-sailing relationship. Possessing the same set of values as you do, a woman is definitely girlfriend material if she gains the respect and approval of your family and friends.

You have awesome chemistry.

A mediocre life is not worth living. Physical attraction is only one aspect of chemistry with another person. You need to be able to understand one another deeply if you want your relationship to last. Your thought styles and personalities need to mesh well with one another, and you should share the same libido (sex-drive) as one another.

She views life with optimism.

A cheerful disposition will undoubtedly endure the test of time while good looks do. In times of hardship and difficulty, positivity is a breath of fresh air, and a kind person will undoubtedly be able to find the positive in every circumstance. Being drama-free and avoiding tense debates and confrontations are other aspects of positivity. The fact that you both feel content in each other's arms at the end of the day is what matters in your relationship.

She has compassion and selflessness for others.

Women's treatment of one another reflects how they view themselves. Treating others with the utmost selflessness only serves to demonstrate that she is aware of and considerate of the needs that each and every individual has.

She gives you the freedom to lead and is always by your side.

She is aware that taking the initiative would help you feel more manly in the relationship. She is also aware that all men desire significant life achievements in order to feel fulfilled. A woman who is a good candidate for a girlfriend should be the very first to encourage you to work toward your objectives, especially during pivotal times when self-doubt seems to rule.

She is a very maternal individual.

You and your partner ought to provide each other with a safe haven. People who are nurturing and caring will make you feel special and loved in small but profound ways, such as by cooking for you or tending to you after a demanding day at work.

She is accountable

You must also make sure that she is dependable and someone you can depend on before starting a new relationship. She also understands how to manage her money wisely and with responsibility. The ideal partner is not also materialistic and understands the value of saving money instead of blowing it all on things like excessive shopping.

She is logical and intelligent.

This applies to informal education as well. If there are difficulties or problems during your relationship, your ideal partner should be someone who is street smart and creative enough to come up with solutions.

She has long-term thinking.

Making plans for the long term as well as the immediate future is part of committing to a relationship. An ideal partner should have the same long-term perspective as you and be able to envision a future with you.

She is adept at caring for herself.

A person's attitude toward herself is also demonstrated by how well she looks after her overall well-being. She is aware that an ideal partnership calls for everyone to be at their best, including their physical well-being. A woman who is girlfriend material maintains her physical fitness by eating well, exercising, and avoiding the party girl lifestyle that could involve alcohol or, worse, drugs. She must also motivate you to lead a healthy lifestyle and partake in a variety of physical activities together.

She only makes advances toward you.

Having a sociable, laid-back girlfriend who makes an effort to get along with your friends is such a pleasure. Despite how cliché it sounds, there is a fine line between being friendly and being flirtatious. If she exerts too much effort with a different man in your life, keep an eye out for her. She must never flirt with any man she encounters along the way for one reason or another.

Her prior heartbreaks have left her totally healed.

This does not imply that she is still close with her ex-boyfriends. Simply put, before entering into a new relationship, a woman must be able to fully and completely heal from all the pain she has previously experienced.

Chapter 2

She is not horrified by your past.

The two of you would eventually get to the point where you felt secure enough to inquire about one another's pasts. A wise lady recognizes that your history shaped who you are now.

She gives you enough breathing room.

a woman who is not overly attached and who recognizes that you both need to take some time apart in order to grow personally and contribute even more to your relationship.

She's not your typical type,

Your ex-lovers are present for a purpose. What purpose would it serve to repeatedly date the same kind of person? If the woman you're dating managed to shatter stereotypes, she is definitely worth your time.

She has the courage to occasionally let loose and act crazy.

A surefire way to assess confidence is to relax. She shouldn't be so self-conscious that it prevents her from trying new things out of fear that other people will judge her for it.

She cares a lot.

Last but not least, think about beginning a relationship with a woman who is not resentful and forgiving of minor transgressions. No relationship is perfect, and she is well aware that any difficulties a couple may face along the way will only strengthen their bond. She is thankful that you two get to overcome these obstacles together as a couple despite the difficulties.

Make a wise choice because your girlfriend will be the one you spend the majority of your time with. Finding someone who meets all of the criteria I've outlined above is incredibly difficult. Finding the ideal match for you should be made easier for you thanks to the information in this article. Avoid the error of accepting less simply to satisfy a void created by your loneliness. Choose the qualities you value most, and keep looking for the right girl until you do.

She has a practical outlook on life.

It was looks first, lifestyle second, and libido third when I was in my teens and early twenties. Now, it's cooking, generosity, good looks, and all-around laid-backness. Fortunately, I've known these people for a very long time, so I don't really worry about dating anymore. I've recently been primarily concerned with bettering my family and myself because it is pretty exhausting.

She only engages in excellent interactions.

"Our interactions account for almost 80% of it. Are we enjoying ourselves by simply conversing? I believe that since this is what we will be doing the majority of the time, we should enjoy it. I can ignore a lot of things if that is going well. But there must be a fundamental draw. Additionally, long-term factors like her strength.

She is self-reliant and logical.

Very effective communication skills. calmness, courtesy, and reason. Kindness and empathy. A joy of attempting new sexual experiences and little to no sexual guilt. Absence of manipulation and drama. realising that I need a certain level of aloneness. She is financially responsible for herself, pays her fair portion for dates, etc.

She has coherent life objectives.

Good character, intelligence (so we can discuss the nature of reality, the cosmos, the soul stone, and other such topics), attractiveness, matching libido, and compatibility with aspirations in life.

To understand how to be the perfect boyfriend material, **read Boyfriend Material: by Valentine Smith to know the qualities of an ideal man.**

www.ingramcontent.com/pod-product-compliance
Lightning Source LLC
LaVergne TN
LVHW052032170826
845678LV00020B/3594

* 9 7 9 8 3 6 7 8 1 7 2 0 1 *